Tim Duncan

by Scott Howard-Cooper

SCHOLASTIC INC.

New York   Toronto   London   Auckland   Sydney
Mexico City   New Delhi   Hong Kong   Buenos Aires

PHOTO CREDITS

All images copyright NBAE/Getty Images
Cover: D. Clarke Evans; (1) Andy Lyons; (2, 3) D. Clarke Evans; (4) Jed Jacobsohn; (6) Chris Covatta; (10) Doug Pensinger; (11) Todd Warshaw; (12) Jonathan Daniel/Stringer (Getty Images); (13) Doug Pensinger (1994 Getty Images); (14) Doug Pensinger (1994 Getty Images); (15) Rick Stewart/Stringer (Getty Images); (17) Craig Jones; (18) Stephen Dunn; (19) Todd Warshaw; (20) NBA Photos; (22) Rocky Widner; (21) David Sherman; (23) D. Clarke Evans; (24) Glenn James; (25) Lou Capozzola; (26) Nathaniel S. Butler; (29) Atiba Jefferson

ISBN 0-439-70398-0

12   11   10   9   8   7   6   5   4   3   5   6   7   8/0

Printed in the U.S.A.
First printing, February 2005
Book Design: Louise Bova

Meet Tim Duncan

Everyone knew Tim Duncan would become a famous athlete one day, but it was supposed to be as a swimmer, the sport he starred in while growing up. Tim didn't start playing basketball until later. Once he did, though, he never stopped.

Duncan grew up on a small island in the U.S. Virgin Islands and went on to become an NBA hero around the world. He has led the San Antonio Spurs to two championships and represented the United States in the Olympics. In addition, he has become one of the most well-liked players in the league. His relaxed personality makes him easy to get along with, while his quiet approach

to the game delivers loud results.

Tim's coach with the Spurs, Gregg Popovich, has said that Duncan's attitude is "remarkable. He's on island time. He puts things in perspective, not adding too much importance, not getting too upbeat or too depressed."

However, don't confuse being relaxed with being too easy on the court. Duncan has been named NBA Most Valuable Player twice. He has developed a reputation as a well-rounded and hard working player. He can score and rebound, and he passes very well. And that's just on offense. On defense, he is considered one of the best power forwards every year. He's difficult to stop on both ends of the floor. He also has great fundamentals. Coaches and teammates love that about Duncan. Opponents know that is what makes him so tough to stop.

Fans appreciate him just as much. Tim is regularly voted in as a starter for the NBA All-Star

game, one sign of how much supporters like him and appreciate his style. He is especially admired in San Antonio, Texas. But that's really no surprise. Tim has played like a superstar and helped bring championships to his adopted city, and the people there welcome him like a family member.

Duncan has treated them just as well. In addition to his work with the Spurs, he spends a lot of his free time with charities including the NBA's Read to Achieve program. With his wife, Amy, he has created an organization to work with community groups in "the areas of health awareness and research, education and youth sport and recreation." Amy Duncan is the

executive vice president of this organization, which is active in San Antonio, as well as in Tim's college home of North Carolina, and his boyhood home in the U.S. Virgin Islands.

Tim raises a lot of money for important causes. One publication, *The Sporting News*, was so impressed by his efforts that it named Duncan one of the "Good Guys" in sports in 2001 *and* 2002. Also in 2001, the NBA honored him with the Home Team Service Award.

In addition to his charity work, Tim knows how to have fun as well — and he's got a quirky sense of humor. For example he likes to wear his practice shorts backward, a trend he started while in college at Wake Forest University. In addition, he has a sword collection, including a three-foot samurai sword. He also loves to play video games — but they shouldn't include sharks! Tim is afraid of sharks and also of heights, even though he is tall himself.

Most of the time, however, it is other teams who are afraid of Tim. Ever since he joined the NBA in 1997–98 and was named Rookie of the Year, Tim has continued to improve. After seven seasons, he still has a bright future — in basketball, not swimming.

Growing Up

Timothy Theodore Duncan was born April 25, 1976, in St. Croix, Virgin Islands, a territory of the United States located in the Caribbean, just east of Puerto Rico. Only about twice the size of Washington, D.C., it is best known for tourism.

Tim didn't grow up playing basketball, his interest was swimming, just as it was for his two sisters, Cheryl and Tricia.

Tricia was so good that she competed in the 1988 Olympics in the 100-meter and 200-meter backstroke. Tim began to show great promise about a year later, when he was 13, especially in the 400-meter freestyle. His times in that event ranked among the top competitors in the United States, and years later the grown-up Duncan would still hold Virgin Islands records in the 50-meter and 100-meter freestyle.

"Timmy was even better than me," Tricia said in a story in *Sports Illustrated* after her brother had become a basketball star. "There is no doubt in my mind that he would have gone to the 1992 Olympics and held his own against the world."

Tragedies in Duncan's life and his homeland, changed everything. Hurricane Hugo struck the island on September 17, 1989, destroying the island's only Olympic-size pool, which Tim would normally use. He was hesitant to swim in the ocean because of the fear of sharks, so, more and more, basketball became his outlet.

Then, shortly before his fourteenth birthday, Tim's mother died from breast cancer. He was so saddened that he gave up competitive swimming for good. Extra attention went to the backboard and pole outside his home that had been a gift from Cheryl, who was living in Ohio. Cheryl eventually moved back to the Virgin Islands with her husband, Ricky Lowery. Rick had a lot of experience playing basketball and began teaching Tim the fundamentals and playing one-on-one games with him.

When Tim grew eight inches, he went from someone who played basketball to someone who commanded attention. It didn't matter that he was living somewhere that didn't get a lot of attention. Or that the island was said to have only four indoor courts, and that those were usually used for volleyball. People began to hear about the rising star with the unique background.

It wasn't the massive publicity that would eventually become part of Tim's everyday life, but it was a lot for a quiet young man and a laid-back island. Coaches from Wake Forest University, Providence College, the University of Hartford, and Delaware State University made the trip to St. Croix to watch Duncan and consider him for a college scholarship. Wake Forest coach Dave Odom was particularly interested after one of Odom's former players was among a group of NBA rookies that played in the Virgin Islands on a tour and reported that Duncan did a solid job on defense against Alonzo Mourning. Everyone knew that Mourning was a college star with a bright future in the pros, so that was quite a compliment.

Odom went to see for himself and was impressed. Then he convinced Duncan to attend Wake Forest. From then on Tim's life would never be the same.

If Duncan was going to remain the same relaxed, quiet young man he had been, playing at Wake Forest would be an immediate test. The school is located in North Carolina, in the town of Winston-Salem, and people there love hoops. The rivalries are strong and the expectations are high. In that immediate area, Duke, North Carolina, and North Carolina State had basketball traditions. That also meant they had pressure to continue to succeed.

It was a complete change for Tim. He went from a place where basketball was not that important to one where it was everything to some people. However, Tim was not expected to make an impact right away. This

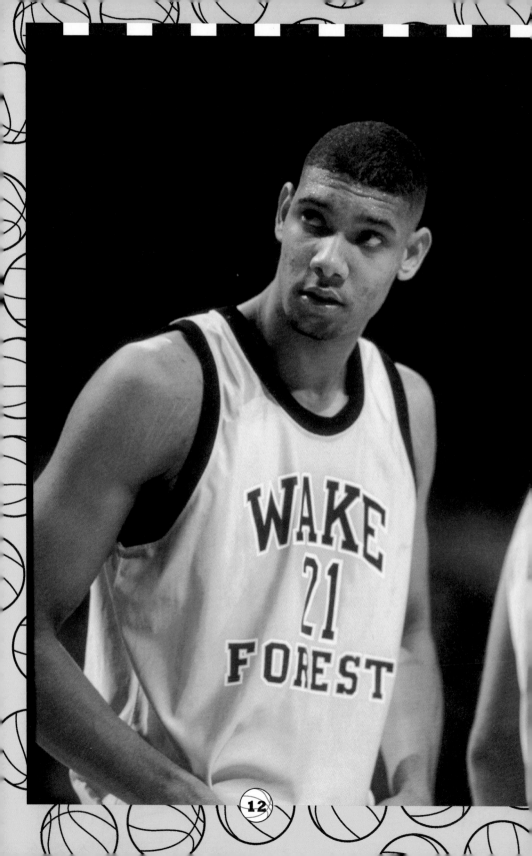

would be the first time he would face this level of competition on a regular basis, so it was supposed to be a quiet beginning. It was — for one game. He didn't score any points or even take any shots in his debut against the University of Alaska-Anchorage.

After that slow start, Duncan developed into a star, especially on defense. He averaged 9.8 points, which isn't bad, but had the biggest impact when he set the school record for blocked shots. And it was only his first season!

His offense was more evident the next year. Tim went from that 9.8 points all the way to 16.8 points in 1993–94 and the Demon Deacons remained one of the best teams in the country. With 16.8 points and 12.5 rebounds, he was one of only two players in the

Atlantic Coast Conference to average double figures in both categories. Just two years into major college competition, he was already a standout.

At a time when many college stars were leaving school early to play in the NBA, Tim chose to stay. Sure, he would have been picked in the draft, but that wasn't the issue. Instead, he followed through on a promise all three Duncan kids had made to their mom: to earn college degrees. Cheryl and Tricia had done it, and now Tim would have his turn.

His final two seasons were the best yet. As a junior, he led Wake Forest to its second league championship in a row. And again he resisted the temptation to go to the pros — even though a lot of people said he would be the top pick in the

whole draft. College meant a lot to him and he meant a lot to the school. Ticket sales and donations increased in Tim's time there, going from an average of 10,496 fans at home games when he first arrived to 14,075 when he left. That's an impressive increase of 34 percent.

As high as the expectations were for his final season, 1996–97, he met them all. He led the country in rebounding that season (14.7 RPG) and was also tenth in blocked shots. In addition, Tim was named the college player of the year by several organizations, including the prestigious Wooden Award that had extra importance because it took academics and character into consideration as well as basketball talent. And he also got his all-important college degree, in psychology.

Coach Odom, in an interview in *Sport* magazine, later summed up Tim's college career. "In my thirty-one years of coaching," the coach said, "I've never met a more fierce competitor, a player who gives you more every day than Tim — in every challenge, whether it be practice, game preparation through film and scouting reports, or the game itself." His decision to leave the Virgin Islands for Wake Forest had been an amazing success and put Tim in perfect position for an even bigger challenge.

This time, unlike college, the expectations were high from the start. Tim was the No. 1 pick in the 1997 NBA Draft and the focus of a lot of attention. People did not just wonder whether he would be as good in San Antonio as he was at Wake Forest. They also wondered about how

well Tim would work with his new teammate, David Robinson.

Robinson was already an established star with the Spurs. Not only that, he played center and Tim would be the power forward. This meant that there could possibly be a conflict in the offense and that the two big men would be going for the same rebounds. A

different pair of players might have had trouble with the arrangement — the new guy wanting to make an impact or the pro wanting to remain the one and only star.

Not them.

"I never thought it wouldn't work," Robinson would say years later. "Especially when you find the right two guys."

And these were the right two guys. Tim told everyone he just wanted to contribute to Robinson's team and get better every day, and The Admiral delighted at Duncan's success. They worked together very well from the start. It probably helped that they had similar personalities: neither man craved attention or had a big ego. Both were smart and had long college careers that

prepared them for the NBA. And both were hard workers.

It became a perfect pairing. Tim was named Rookie of the Year in 1997–98. Not only that, he became the first rookie since Larry Bird to be named first-team All-NBA, a selection that immediately ranked him as one of the top players in the game. Spending four years in college, as opposed to so many other hopeful stars who left school early, and being four years more mature was paying off.

Duncan averaged 21.1 points, 11.9 rebounds, 2.7 assists, and 2.51 blocks that season. He also led all first-year players in just about every statistical category and played in the NBA All-Star game. Robinson, meanwhile, remained a star. As both predicted, and opponents feared, they were capable of greatness even while playing on the same team.

"I think it was limiting at first, but I think we've found ways to feed off each other instead of get in each other's way," Duncan said. "When we play well, we *both* play well. It's not because one guy plays well. It's because we're helping each other."

That part would never change. David Robinson and Tim Duncan clearly trusted each other on the court and they learned to feed off each other, but a change was coming. Robinson was 33 when the 1998–99 season started, and he sensed it was time to move aside and let his younger teammate become the undisputed star. Most of the rest of the Spurs were like that as well. It was a roster that worked very well together. The entire team in search of one goal: An NBA title.

There was nothing ordinary about the 1998 season, Tim's second season. It was a special season for Tim and the Spurs, one that would forever remain in the hearts of San Antonio fans everywhere. The Spurs won its first championship since joining the NBA in 1976–77.

Tim had become the best of the best. He was only 23, but he was named first-team All-NBA *and* first-team All-Defense. He was young but he had already become an established star with a long future ahead of him. Robinson took a supporting role without complaint and Duncan was named the NBA

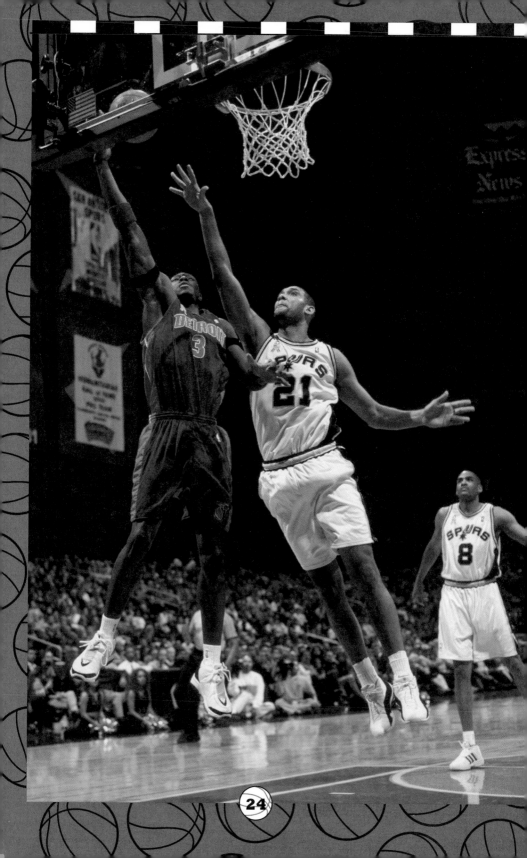

Finals Most Valuable Player after the Spurs beat the New York Knicks in five games. The most famous picture from that moment, though, was of the two players standing side by side while hoisting the trophies overhead.

When Duncan hurt his knee, San Antonio's hopes of a repeat championship in 2000 were ruined. But that proved to be the only thing that could slow him down. When he was healthy again, Tim was a force, as every opponent knew. He went from averaging 21.1 and 21.7 points his first two seasons, to climbing to 23.2. A slight dip to 22.2 followed, and then he went all the way to 25.5 in 2001–02.

Even as all the achievements came, he maintained the same laid-back personality. Success did not spoil him. It seemed like nothing could. In the same season he broke the 25-point barrier, Tim also led the league in total rebounds (1,042) and scored

more baskets (764) than anyone. He was named the regular-season Most Valuable Player, one of the few awards that had previously eluded him. Tim was also becoming a regular on the international scene, playing for the United States in tournaments to qualify for the Olympics.

He called representing his country in those competitions an honor. Tim's primary focus, though, remained on San Antonio and another NBA crown. He wouldn't have to wait long.

The 2002–03 regular season finished with Tim named MVP again, making him just the eighth player ever to win the award two years in a row. He was just as good, if not better, in the playoffs. The Spurs won the title for the second time and Tim set a record with 32 blocks in the final round against the New Jersey Nets. He had eight of those in one game alone, another record.

Robinson retired after that season, ending a great career. Another career continued: Tim averaged 22.3 points and 12.4 rebounds in 2003–04 and was named first-team All-NBA for the seventh year in a row. In other words, *every* season since he had turned pro.

After what would have qualified as a successful career for most players, Tim strived for more. He went into the summer of 2004 with a lot of big plans for the future. He was one of the leaders of the U.S. team in Athens, Greece, and played in the Olympics for the first time, helping the U.S. win the bronze medal. (A knee injury had knocked him out of the 2000 Games in Sydney, Australia.) Tim is in his prime, which is bad news for the rest of the NBA. As long as he is wearing No. 21, the Spurs will continue to be top contenders for the NBA title. Both Tim and the Spurs are ready for more championships.